MISTAKES THAT PRODUCED SCIENTIFIC ADVANCEMENTS

Science Book 6th Grade

Children's How Things Work Books

BABY PROFESSOR

EDUCATION KIDS

In this book, we're going to talk about mistakes that produced scientific advancements. So, let's get right to it!

Scientists are always creating new inventions or advancements in science. However, sometimes something happens by accident and it leads in a totally different direction than the scientist is researching.

These "happy accidents" led to new inventions for the scientists who realized that their results were just as interesting as what they were trying to do in the first place!

THE TEFLON PAN

Roy Plunkett was tinkering with chlorofluorocarbon (CFC) gases, because he was trying to create a new type of refrigerant. He was storing some gas cylinders that contained a gas called tetrafluoroethylene. He packed the cylinders in dry ice because the gas was volatile and he didn't want it to explode in the laboratory where he was working.

Teflon Pan

However, when he went back to get the gas to use it in his experiments, he discovered that it had transformed into flakes that were waxy and white. This interesting new substance was very slippery, but it was also stable. He discovered that it was amazingly resistant. He could hit it with heat or acid and throw it under water and it all seemed to just roll off.

It wasn't clear what possible use this unusual substance could have until a French engineer by the name of Marc Grégoire figured out how to affix the substance to aluminum. The result was the very first pan with a non-stick surface and the brand called "Teflon" was soon launched.

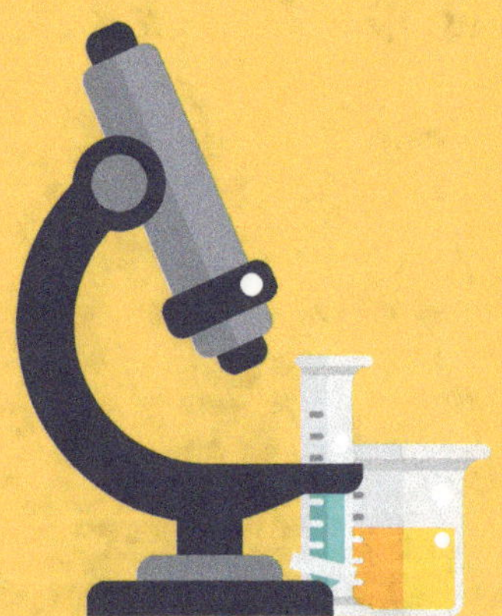

Microwave Oven

THE MICROWAVE OVEN

Percy Spencer worked for Raytheon. The company was a defense contractor for the United States military during World War II. Percy was working at the radiation lab at the Massachusetts Institute of Technology in 1946. As senior engineer, he was trying to develop a magnetron that had more power. The magnetron was a vacuum tube that was an integral piece of the radar devices.

He was hungry and had a chocolate bar in his pocket that he was going to eat. He was close to the front of one of his test magnetrons when he noticed that something unusual had happened. The chocolate bar had melted and the lab wasn't hot. He went to get a bag of popcorn that wasn't popped to see if the machine would pop the corn and it did!

That's how the microwave oven was invented. The next year Raytheon's enormous-sized "Radarange" went on sale. Today it's rare for people not to have at least one microwave in their homes. It saves so much time for busy working people who want to create quick meals.

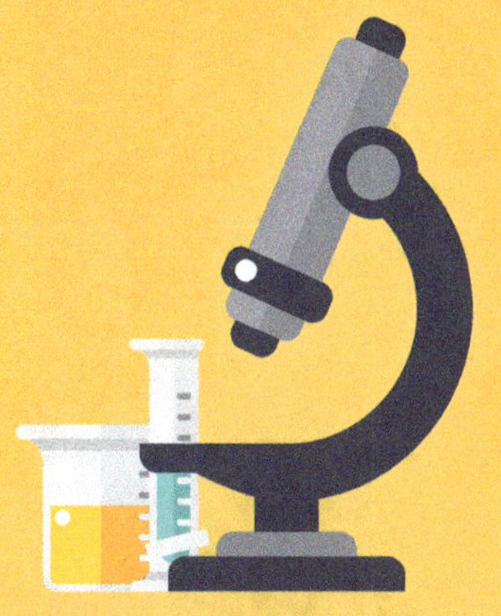

SYNTHETIC DYE

William Perkin was a lab assistant in London in 1864. The eighteen-year-old had been assigned to try and figure out another way for creating quinine. Quinine is an expensive drug used to combat malaria. One of his attempts that had failed produced something strange at the bottom of a beaker. It was a vibrant purple sludge that was a more intense color than was found in nature.

Synthetic Dye

Curious about the weird sludge, Perkin worked with it and discovered that he had created an artificial dye. This discovery led to a huge industry dedicated to the creation of synthetic dyes.

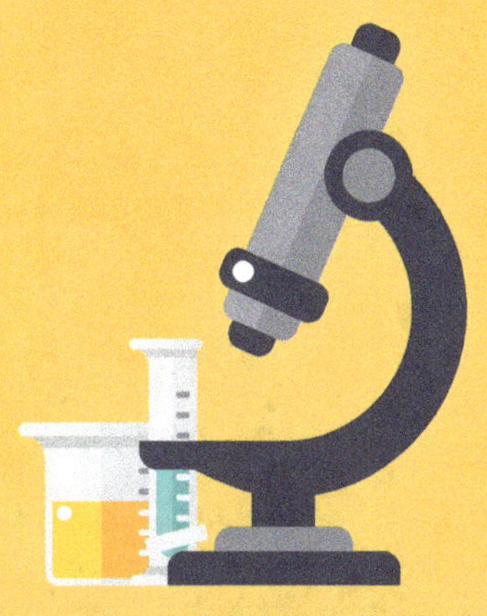

THE PACEMAKER

Have you ever reached into a toolbox without looking and pulled out the wrong tool? That's what happened to an inventor by the name of Wilson Greatbatch. The result of this mistake was an invention that's saved hundreds of thousands of lives.

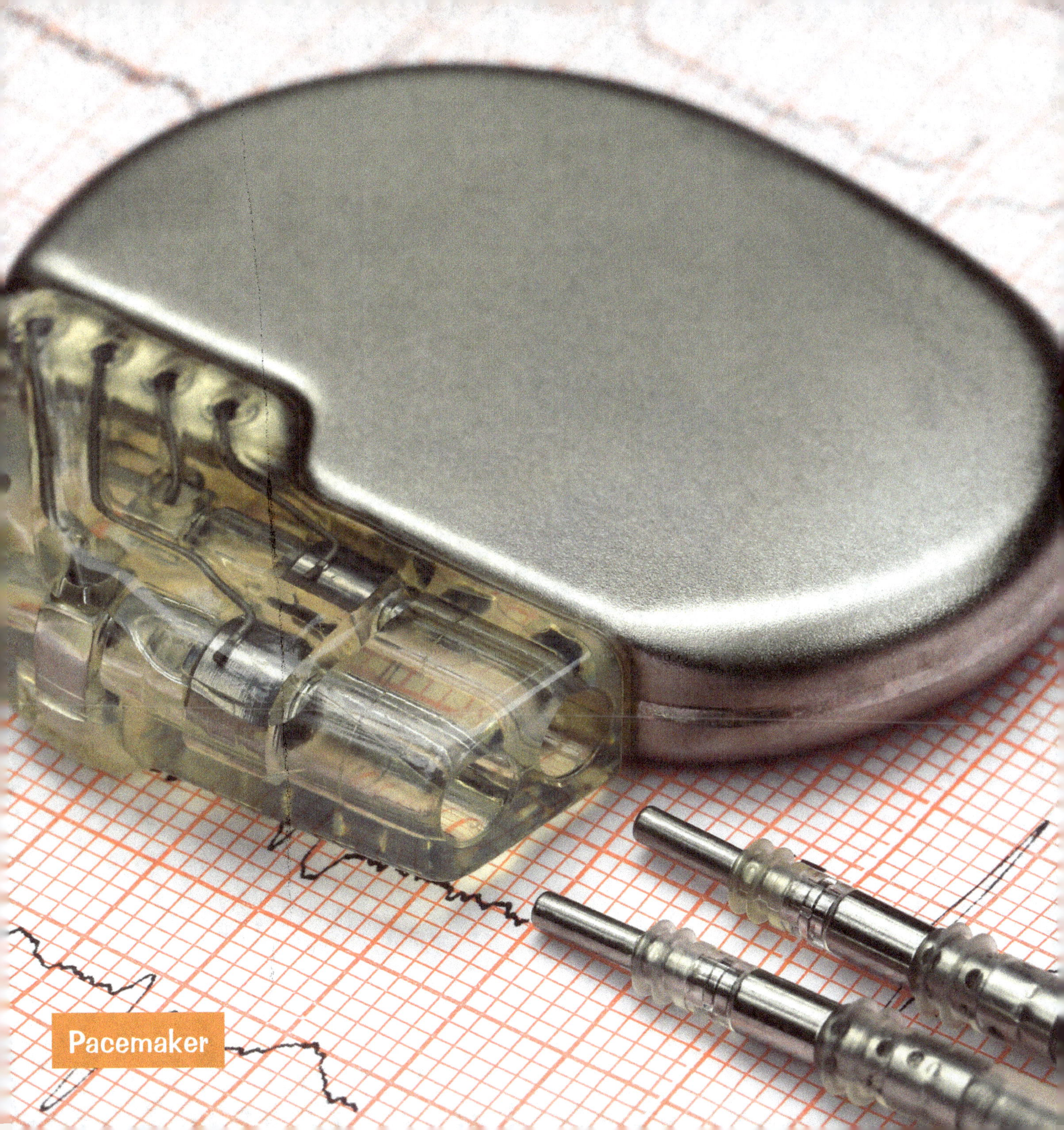
Pacemaker

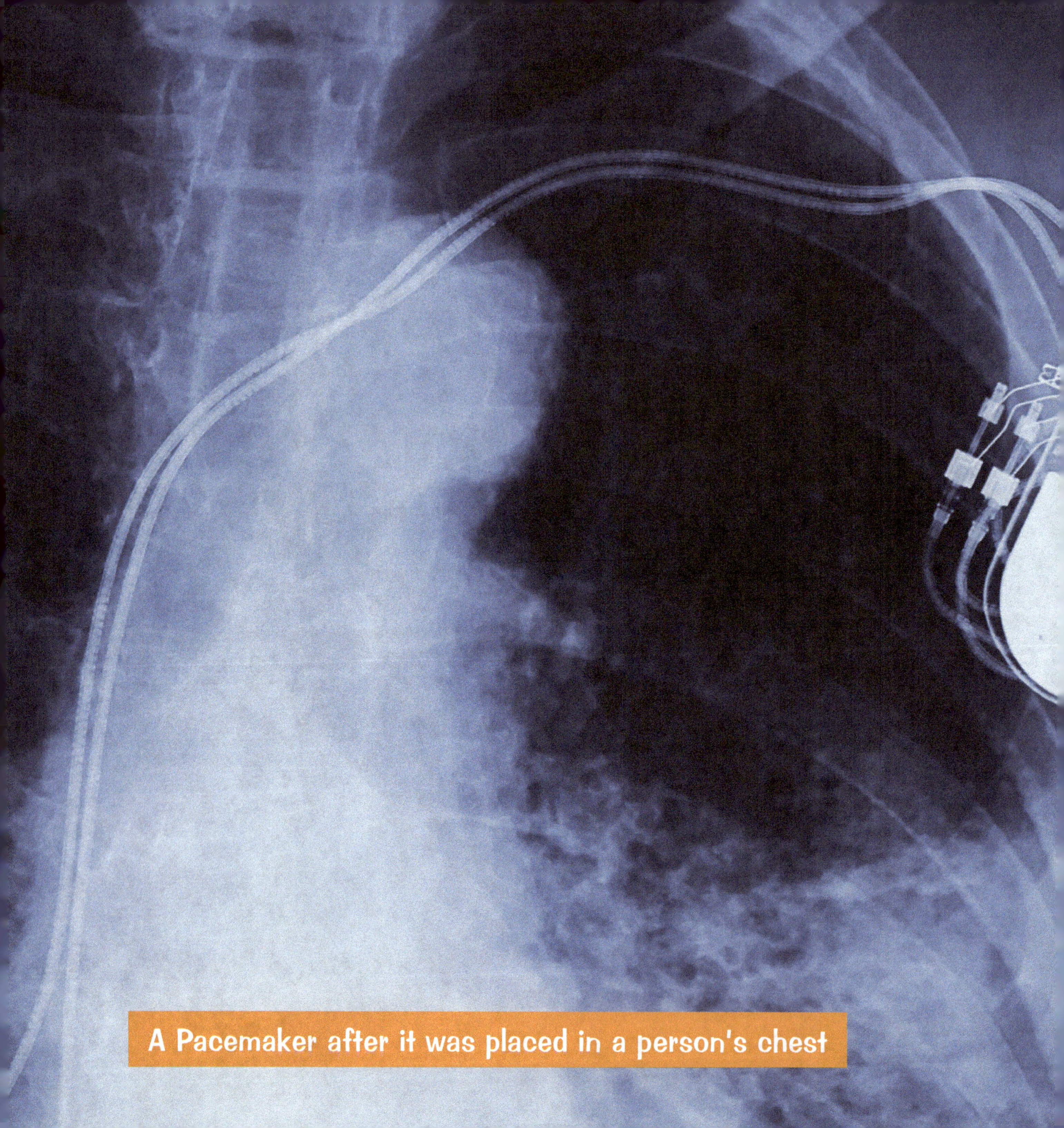

A Pacemaker after it was placed in a person's chest

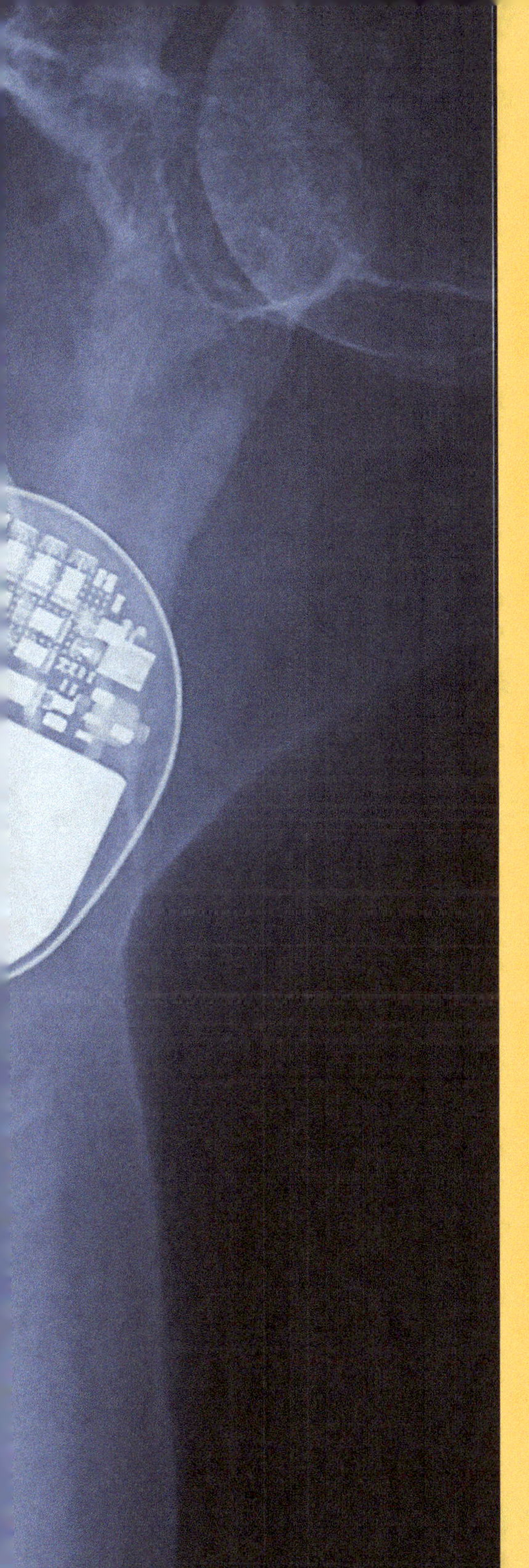

Greatbatch was hard at work attempting to make a circuit for the purpose of recording heartbeats that were too fast. However, he grabbed a resistor that was 1-megaohm instead of the 10,000-megaohm one he needed for the circuit. The product he ended up with pulsed for just 1.8 milliseconds, then stopped for a full second and repeated its pulse.

The scientist realized that his circuit was emulating a human heartbeat! The discovery led to the initial version of the pacemaker. In 1960, the first pacemaker was placed inside a 77-year-old man and he lived for another year and a half after he received the device.

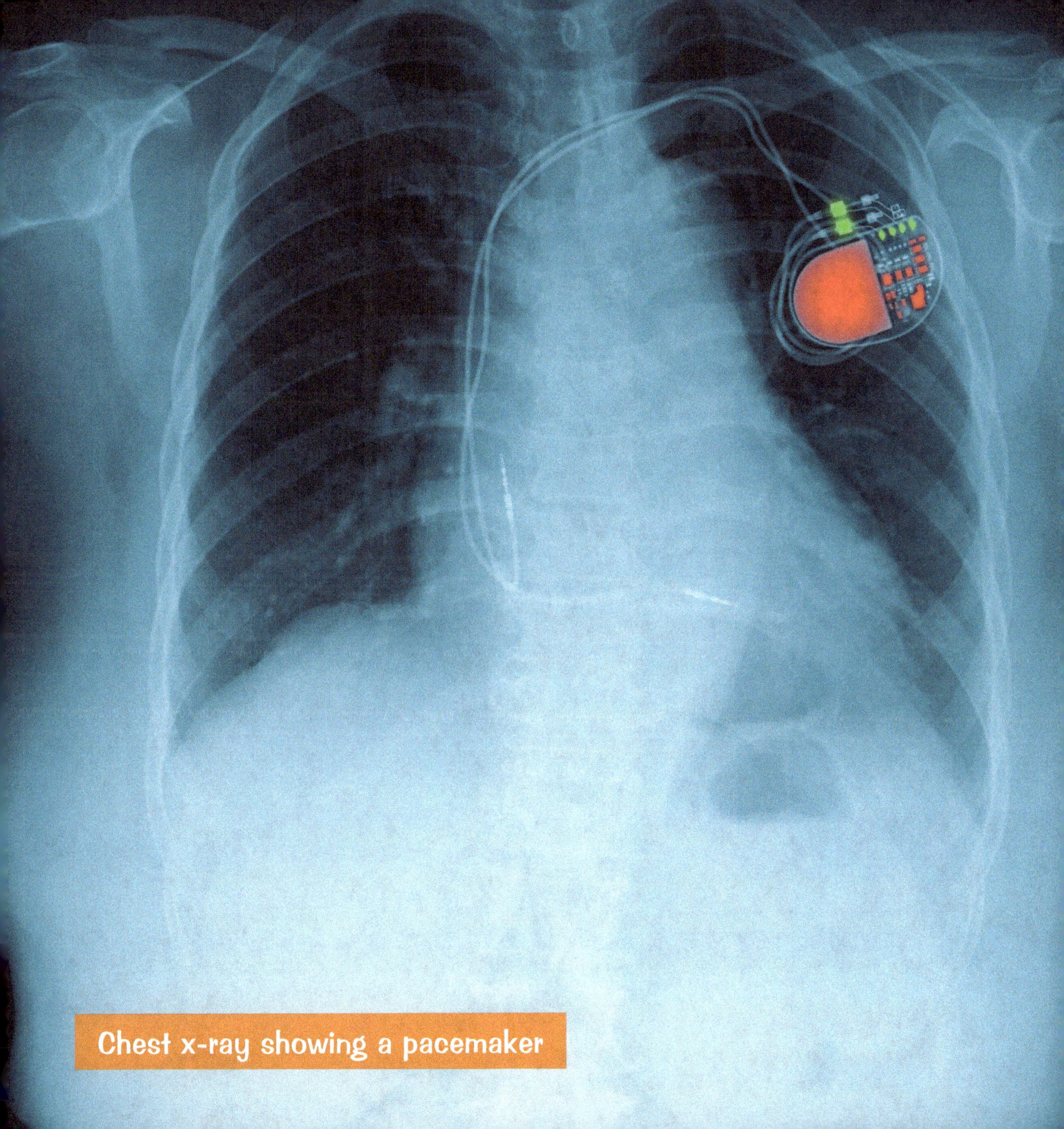

Chest x-ray showing a pacemaker

The Karl G. Jansky Very Large Array (VLA)

RADIO ASTRONOMY

In 1931, an engineer by the name of Karl Jansky was trying to find out why there was so much interference in the sound when people were using telephone lines. After some investigation it was found that celestial bodies in space were causing the problem! The science of radio astronomy happened because of this discovery.

Thirty years later, two engineers working with radio, Arno Penzias and his colleague Robert Wilson were trying to find out what was causing a hissing sound they were hearing. What they had found by accident was the remnants of the Big Bang, the gigantic explosion that started the universe. That hissing sound was from radiation from the first cosmic microwaves. It was still hissing away at the background of the universe after billions of years.

radio astronomy observatory

TEXT MESSAGING

In 1987, a team in Europe was setting up new standards for cellular phones. The designs for smaller mobile phones that would be more easily portable were in the works. The design team wanted a standard system that would work across the entire European continent so that there would be a spirit of harmony and cooperation among countries.

In the script, there was a way for the telecommunication engineers to send quick messages between the teams so they could manage the network for the phones. They were so surprised when consumers found out about the "Short Message Service."

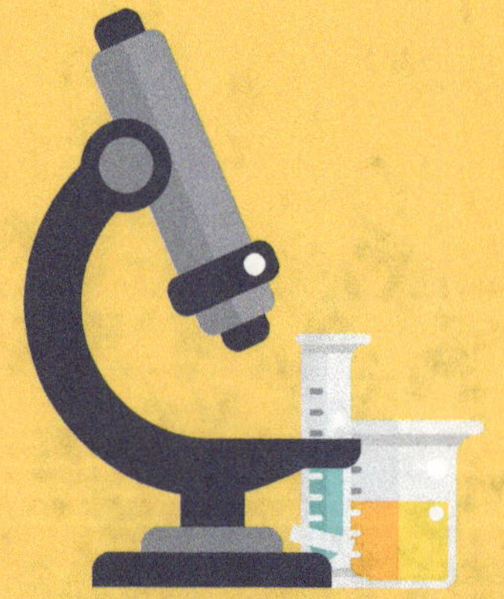

DUALBAND
MENU
YES
NO
CLR

They wanted to use it for themselves! SMS was born and millions of us across the world now use it on our phones every day.

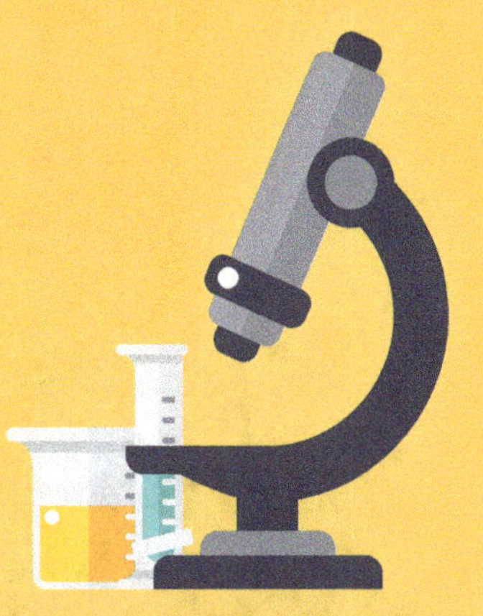

X-RAYS

Wilhelm Röntgen was hard at work in his laboratory at the University of Würzberg in 1895. He was researching cathode rays and their properties. He was using a special screen of barium platinocyanide when he saw a strange glow from the corner of his eye.

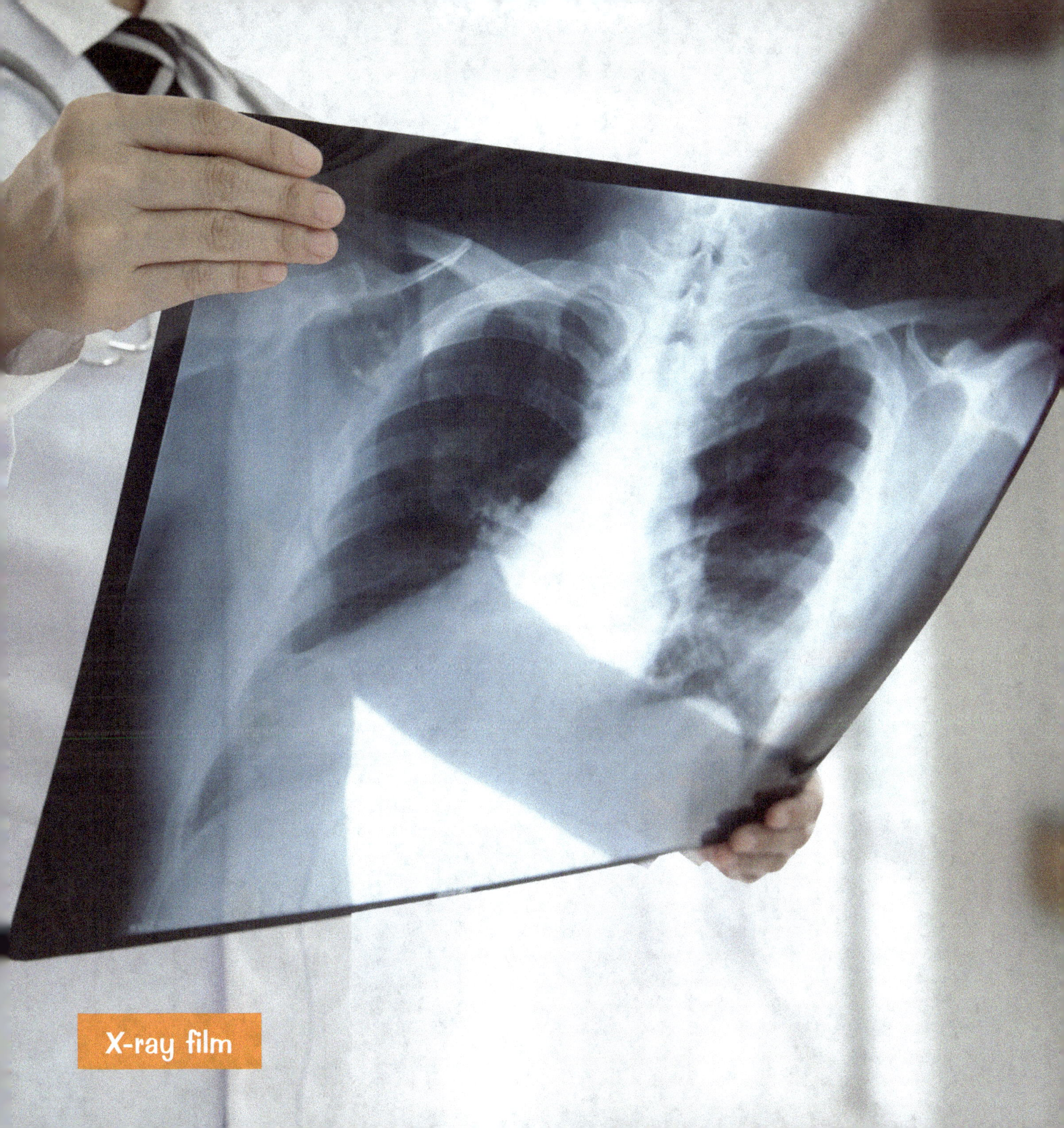
X-ray film

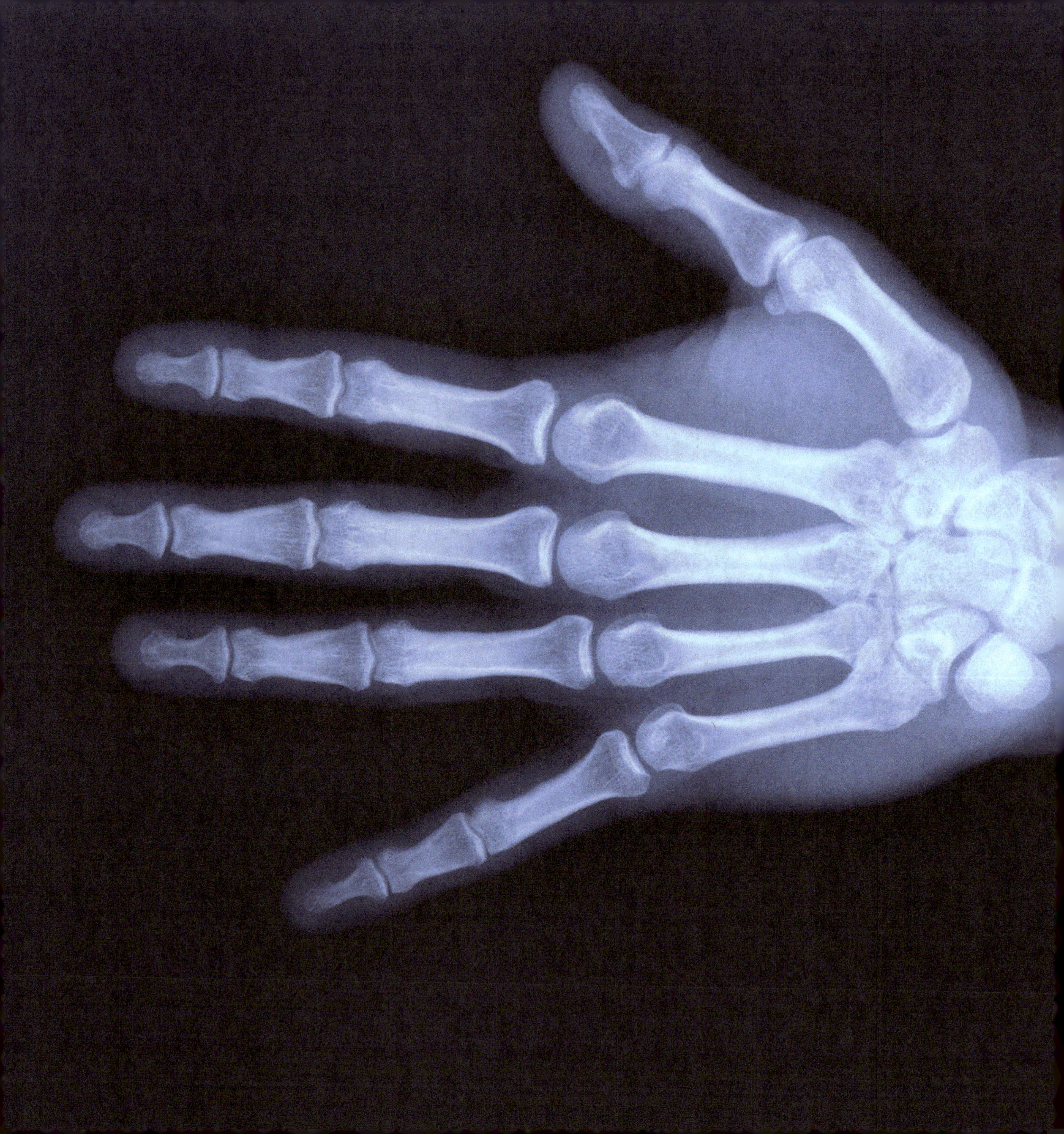

Imagine how shocked he was when he saw the bones inside his hand. He realized that something mysterious was passing in the air and was casting a shadow on the screen. The strange "X-rays" were created in other laboratories worldwide and twenty years later they were being used for an array of applications in medicine.

SACCHARIN

You should always wash your hands when working with chemicals! However, Contantin Fahlberge didn't do that in 1878 and the result was a sweet success. He was working at Johns Hopkins University and experimenting with new forms of coal tar. He went home after working in the lab and was surprised that everything he ate was much sweeter than usual.

Artificial sweetener

Saccharin

He raced back to his lab and tasted the contents of all the evaporating dishes he was using until he found the sweet substance. It was saccharin. It's a good thing that none of the other substances he tasted were poisonous!

SUPERGLUE

Harry Coover was the head of a team at Eastman Kodak. The chemist and his team were trying to invent a clear plastic. Their work was happening during World War II and the purpose of the plastic was to develop gun sights that were transparent.

Superglue

One of their failed attempts made a strange gloop that stuck to every different item that it touched. They had created cyanoacrylate by accident. Coover soon found out that this amazing new substance had a strange property.

It could bond together in a very sticky mess when there was moisture present. The scientific term for this process is polymerization. Their team had created a type of glue that was amazingly strong but didn't need heat or any pressure to do its bonding work.

rainbow slinky

THE SLINKY

Richard James had a tough problem to solve in 1943. He was attempting to build a type of spring that would help the sensitive devices and instruments on ships from rocking so hard that they wouldn't function properly anymore. He was working away when he elbowed one of his prototypes. Instead of just crashing on the floor, the prototype did something unusual. It sprang downward gracefully and then was able to right itself!

The spring's nimble behavior was so pointless and yet there was something really fun about it. This accident eventually resulted in one of the best-selling toys ever. Richard's wife named the toy "Slinky" and over 300 million have been sold. Kids just loved and still love the silly toy. Have you ever tried to get a slinky to go all the way to the bottom of the stairs?

SUMMARY

Throughout the history of modern science, scientists have used the Scientific Method to create experiments so they can develop new inventions and advance the cause of science. However, many amazing scientific discoveries have been "happy accidents" that led to incredible inventions that no one had yet dreamed of.

Awesome! Now that you know more about mistakes that produced scientific advancements you may want to read about the Scientific Method in the Baby Professor book What is the Scientific Method? Science Book for Kids.

Visit

www.BabyProfessorBooks.com

to download Free Baby Professor eBooks
and view our catalog of new and exciting
Children's Books